© **THOUGHTS MAKE YOU WORK**
BY SANDEEP RAVIDUTT SHARMA

Table of Contents

Foreword IV

Thoughts make you work...1

© **THOUGHTS MAKE YOU WORK**
BY SANDEEP RAVIDUTT SHARMA

Foreword

This book provides you with a list of 100 motivational quotes and thoughts about **LIFE**, churned out by my mind with the consciousness, grace and energy of **Shiva Shakti**. I'm sure if you keep reading, referring, sharing these thoughts and quotes about LIFE, you may derive inspiration, develop positive outlook and good understanding of various perspectives about life. Train your mind to attract and retain good thoughts. It's your thought that weaves the world around you, and guide you as to how to live happily, even when you don't have a single penny.

"Innovations keep happening because thoughts are always at work. Let your thoughts make you work towards creating a better and happy world."

I sincerely hope, you will find this book amazing, interesting, rejuvenating, unique and a constant source of inspiration.

Thank You and Happy Reading.

© THOUGHTS MAKE YOU WORK
BY SANDEEP RAVIDUTT SHARMA

© Copyright 2018 Sandeep Ravidutt Sharma - All rights reserved.
In no way is it legal to reproduce, duplicate, or transmit any part of this document in either electronic means or in printed format. Recording of this publication is strictly prohibited and any storage of this document is not allowed unless with written permission from the publisher. All rights reserved. The information provided herein is stated to be truthful and consistent, in that any liability, in terms of inattention or otherwise, by any usage or abuse of any policies, processes, or directions contained within is the solitary and utter responsibility of the recipient reader. Under no circumstances will any legal responsibility or blame be held against the author / publisher for any reparation, damages, or monetary loss due to the information herein, either directly or indirectly. The author own all copyrights.

Legal Notice:
This book is copyright protected. This is only for personal use. You cannot amend, distribute, sell, use, quote or paraphrase any part or the content within this book without the consent of the author or copyright owner. Legal action will be pursued if this is breached.

Disclaimer Notice:
Please note the information contained within this book is for motivational, educational and knowledge sharing purpose only. Every attempt has been made to provide the reader accurate, up to date and reliable complete information. No warranties of any kind are expressed or implied. Readers acknowledge that the author is not engaging in the rendering of legal, financial, medical or professional advice. By reading this document, the reader agrees that under no circumstances the author / publisher is responsible for any losses, direct or indirect, which are incurred as a result of the use of information contained within this document, including, but not limited to, —errors, omissions, or inaccuracies.

If you have further questions, contact on Tel: **+919969256731**
Email: **sandeepraviduttsharma@gmail.com**

© **THOUGHTS MAKE YOU WORK**
BY SANDEEP RAVIDUTT SHARMA

Dedication

This book is dedicated to **Shiva Shakti** - the epitome of love. Lord Shiva is pure consciousness symbolising the masculine principle. Goddess Shakti symbolises the active feminine energy of Shiva and is synonymously identified with Tripura Sundari, Sati or Parvati.
These primal principles are also called as Purusha representing consciousness and Prakriti denoting the nature. **Shiva** and **Shakti** are manifestations of the all-in-one divine consciousness. Shiva is the paternal love of God that gives us consciousness, knowledge and clarity. Shakti is the motherly love of God that showers warmth, care and ensures our protection. Shiva and Shakti exist within each of us as the masculine and feminine energy. To please Shiva Shakti praying for the well being, love, happiness, strength, positive energy and success of my readers in their life, I hereby recite the following mantra...

"Sarva Mangala Mangalye Shive Sarvartha Sadhike Sharanye Tryambake Gauri Narayani Namostute"

Thoughts make you work

© **THOUGHTS MAKE YOU WORK**
BY SANDEEP RAVIDUTT SHARMA

Step out of your comfort zone if you really want to win.

Good character is not just for display but speaks a lot when you act and make difference in the life of the others.

© **THOUGHTS MAKE YOU WORK**
BY SANDEEP RAVIDUTT SHARMA

Stars twinkle to make you happy while Lightning illuminates the Sky to create fear in your heart. Choice is all yours whether to become a Star or Lightning.

Drag the fear of failure out of your mind by focusing only on giving your best and not thinking too much about the result.

Evacuate your life from the summit of loneliness and place it on the shore of happiness to meet the rushing waves of togetherness.

© THOUGHTS MAKE YOU WORK
BY SANDEEP RAVIDUTT SHARMA

You can become the Sun among the dazzling Stars only through your brilliant performance.

Invest in your own self through learning and applying what you have learned in the real world.

You can always make a remark but try not the one which may hurt others.

© **THOUGHTS MAKE YOU WORK**
BY SANDEEP RAVIDUTT SHARMA

Don't try to nail a Mountain when you can't even reach the top. Set realistic goals in life.

Don't expect what doesn't belong to you. And what belongs to you doesn't need any expectations.

The hand of God can be seen by those who remember him always.

Nothing lives better than joy in our Lives.

The amazing world waits for you to cheer up and lead.

© THOUGHTS MAKE YOU WORK
BY SANDEEP RAVIDUTT SHARMA

Channel your aggression towards making a goal in a game instead of converting it into trash talk.

© **THOUGHTS MAKE YOU WORK**
BY SANDEEP RAVIDUTT SHARMA

Hope for the best and give your best to keep up the hope.

Don't Google for happiness but make sincere efforts to find within.

© THOUGHTS MAKE YOU WORK
BY SANDEEP RAVIDUTT SHARMA

Wonderful are the ways of the Lord. The contrasting elements like the Sun and Ocean co-exist peacefully in this Universe when they could have wiped out the other. The sun could have dried up the Ocean, or mighty Ocean could have extinguished the Sun. But they co-exist for billions of years with the grace of the Lord. Let's learn to live and let live peacefully.

Admire the wonderful world through your beautiful eyes and joyful mind.

Don't look for logic in everything. Look beyond and you can explore the realm of the Lord who created everything.

Nothing works better than your sincere efforts.

Relationships sour when we try to force our WILL on to the other without making them understand.

Words influence your actions only when you listen. Those who listen are sure to understand the value of the words spoken.

> © **THOUGHTS MAKE YOU WORK**
> BY SANDEEP RAVIDUTT SHARMA

Don't withdraw unless you intend to come back recharged.

© **THOUGHTS MAKE YOU WORK**
BY SANDEEP RAVIDUTT SHARMA

Standing tall gives you the opportunity to see the world and not to raise your false ego which can make you fall.

Most of us crave to relax under the shade. Why not make effort to become the tree that gives the shade.

The storm in your life will pass over soon. Hold on to your patience and keep up the hope alive.

© **THOUGHTS MAKE YOU WORK**
BY SANDEEP RAVIDUTT SHARMA

People who like you will always be ready to share your joy and sorrow. But if the ones who fought with you are doing it that would mean they liked your character.

You walk in with joyfulness bundled with your sweet smile.

Time seems to be infinite when you live each moment.

Desires can fly without wings but efforts need knowledge to take off.

Array of lights are not required to thwart darkness, one small Candle is good enough to do the same.

Build a Skyscraper but not over the foundation of a hut.

Avoid constant criticism and learn how to appreciate good things in life.

Sometimes one win is enough to wipe out all the losses.

© **THOUGHTS MAKE YOU WORK**
BY SANDEEP RAVIDUTT SHARMA

Why forget in the first place when you need to remember it. Make it your way of life.

Don't assume support but appreciate when someone extends it just for you.

Anticipate the next move and be ready with your plan if you want to win over your competitor.

Kind people never wait for someone to acknowledge their kindness.

Mark the end of inaction if you want to start again.

Fight out negativity by constantly favouring positive thoughts.

Accept your ignorance with a vow to pursue knowledge.

Get going if you have decided to scale the summit.

Amazing World always exist. All you have to do is, train your mind to feel the amazement.

Look at brighter things in life or else you run the risk of attracting darkness and ignorance.

> © **THOUGHTS MAKE YOU WORK**
> BY SANDEEP RAVIDUTT SHARMA

If you are rich, you don't have to convince others that they are poor or less rich than you.

Never mind if someone has crossed the limits just to make you feel happy.

© **THOUGHTS MAKE YOU WORK**
BY SANDEEP RAVIDUTT SHARMA

Don't lose touch with the ground even when you are used to flying.

Set goals in life with the intention and dedication to achieve.

© **THOUGHTS MAKE YOU WORK**
BY SANDEEP RAVIDUTT SHARMA

Truth favours the brave.

With folded hands and gracious Smile let's welcome the change.

Pleasing others won't take you far in life.

Get going right from the first step if you want to see the Sun rise of your life.

© THOUGHTS MAKE YOU WORK
BY SANDEEP RAVIDUTT SHARMA

Soothing music brings in life to meet joyfulness and unclutter your thoughtfulness.

Joyful mind has no place left for pain and suffering.

The wonderful world owes it to your beautiful acceptance of good things in life.

Treat yourself well.

© **THOUGHTS MAKE YOU WORK**
BY SANDEEP RAVIDUTT SHARMA

Nobody can dare to point fingers at you if you have maintained your integrity throughout.

Reading and understanding combine to form knowledge.

Stop arguing with the other if you see it going towards infinity. Choose silence over argument.

Build consensus before making it a law.

Don't forget to motivate those who taught you to laugh.

Don't declare the outcome to yourself before you make the real call.

Hold your tears before they decide to roll down and get lost. Train them to become Pearls of wisdom that can clean your conscience.

Thrash the challenges before you take off.

Life throws surprises and amuses you.

Be the stick that helps one walk and not beat someone causing pain.

It's our flaws and attempt to remove them continuously that makes us human.

Your protest can ignite a revolution. Step forward and lead.

Illusion is no more when you surrender everything to the Lord.

Nothing cures better than your faith.

When you look into the eyes of the failure to understand, you can see the glimpse of the future win.

Instead of finding ways to dry the rain why not build a reservoir.

Let the thought of a beautiful world enrich your mind and bring in the innovation.

Commit yourself to a noble cause without waiting for others to lead.

Rise to the occasion and unleash your talent.

Let the excitement build up to see what the new day has brought for you.

Learn to get along with people who keep motivating everyone either through their deeds or words.

Commitment is fine but in your excitement don't overcommit.

Commitment, plan, efforts, honesty can make you successful, only when action carries them together for you.

How do you handle success counts more than the success itself?

Poverty of ideas are no more when positive thoughts dominate your mind.

Think to create and not delete.

Look for facts and not just assume.

Looking forward doesn't mean crushing others in your pursuit of happiness. But lighting the lamp for others to follow smoothly.

Desire to win is not enough unless backed by innovative efforts.

Not everyone who wanders is lost. Few become torchbearers for others to explore by mapping the path.

© **THOUGHTS MAKE YOU WORK**
BY SANDEEP RAVIDUTT SHARMA

The breakthrough awaits a thoughtful mind.

Don't promise if you have already made up your mind to break it someday.

The winner never does what everyone else is doing. Think and do differently.

With your action and words you can build as well as lose trust. Choose wisely.

Fortunate are those for whom path is already laid to reach their destination. Rare are those who carve their own path before they walk.

© THOUGHTS MAKE YOU WORK
BY SANDEEP RAVIDUTT SHARMA

Great dreams are achieved by ordinary people with extraordinary effort.

Curiosity is in born. All you have to do is encourage to question.

Flight to prosperity is not always direct.

You have the right to share your beliefs but not force it.

Joy and grief follow each other at all times. All you have to do is persuade joy to stay back so that pain keeps waiting.

Fortunate are those including yours truly who get a companion for life who shares both joy and sorrow with you.

Fear goes out of the window when you start discussing with courage.

Those who decide to live in the Clouds forget that one day they will have to touch the ground when it rains.

Nothing succeeds better than your smile.

www.ingramcontent.com/pod-product-compliance
Lightning Source LLC
Chambersburg PA
CBHW020545220526
45463CB00006B/2195